THE TEEN'S MUSICAL THEATRE COLLECTION

YOUNG MEN'S EDITION

Compiled by Louise Lerch

HAL•LEONARD® CORPORATION

7777 W. BLUEMOUND RD. P.O. BOX 13819 MILWAUKEE, WI 53213

For all works contained herein:
Unauthorized copying, arranging, adapting, recording or public performance is an infringement of copyright.
Infringers are liable under the law.

Visit Hal Leonard Online at
www.halleonard.com

CONTENTS

YOUNG MEN'S EDITION • NOTES ON THE SONGS

All I Need Is the Girl from *Gypsy* (1959, Broadway). Tulsa is a dancer in a vaudeville act on the road. In secret he has been working on his own new routine and plans to strike out on his own. In this scene, he tells June his big ideas.

Alone at the Drive-In Movie from *Grease* (1972, Broadway). Danny and Sandy are at the drive-in where Danny tells Sandy he wants to go steady. He then proceeds to make a pass at her, and she is offended and deserts him. He is left alone singing this song.

The Bare Necessities from *The Jungle Book* (1965, film). Baloo, the singing bear, sings about his philosophy of life to Mowgli, a boy who is lost in the Jungle.

Brush Up Your Shakespeare from *Kiss Me, Kate* (1948, Broadway). Two gangsters arrive at a theatre to collect money due them from one of the play's members. They find out that the debt has been canceled and try to leave. On their way out, they make a wrong turn and end up on the stage where they sing this incidental song for the "audience."

Close Every Door from *Joseph and the Amazing Technicolor Dreamcoat* (1976, Off-Broadway; 1981, Broadway). Joseph has been betrayed by his eleven brothers and sold into slavery. He tries to stay hopeful in "Close Every Door."

Everybody Ought to Have a Maid from *A Funny Thing Happened on the Way to the Forum* (1962, Broadway). This show is a broad comedy based on ancient Roman plays. Senex, a citizen of Rome, and Pseudolus, a slave in his home, sing this bawdy song about a pretty young housemaid.

The Farmer and the Cowman from *Oklahoma!* (1943, Broadway). This show takes place in the territory of Oklahoma around 1900. This song is an entertaining ensemble that portrays the eternal conflict between the farmer and the rancher.

Friend Like Me from *Aladdin* (1993, film). Aladdin has stumbled onto a magic lamp. Out pops an amazing genie who sings this song.

Guys and Dolls from *Guys and Dolls* (1950, Broadway). This show takes place in New York among gamblers and racketeers. Two of the lowlifes comically point out what men will do to impress a woman.

He Is an Englishman from *HMS Pinafore* (1878, London). As Josephine, the captain's daughter, and Ralph, the mere seaman, prepare to elope against the captain's wishes, the captain tries to intervene. Ralph uses this song as a response which earns him time in the ship's dungeon cell.

Leaning on a Lamp-Post from *Me and My Girl* (1986, Broadway). "Me and My Girl," an English musical comedy originally produced in 1937 in London, was successfully revived in London and New York in the 1980s. It is a very light, entertaining show, and this song illustrates that.

Les Poissons from *The Little Mermaid* (1989, film). Prince Erik's chef is preparing a meal for himself and Ariel, and Sebastian, the crab friend of Ariel, has accidentally been caught in the kitchen and is trying to escape the chef.

Love, I Hear from *A Funny Thing Happened on the Way to the Forum* (1962, Broadway). Hero is a young man in ancient Rome who has fallen in love for the very first time with a beautiful slave girl.

Luck Be a Lady from *Guys and Dolls* (1950, Broadway). Sky Masterson has bet on the roll of the dice that, if he wins, the losers will pay him not in money but with their souls. They will have to show up at the Salvation Army prayer meeting, which keeps the mission open and his girlfriend Sarah happy and in the neighborhood.

My Defenses Are Down from *Annie Get Your Gun* (1946, Broadway). Frank Butler, a sharpshooter and performer in a Wild West show, has fallen in love with the unladylike Annie Oakley, much to his surprise.

On the Street Where You Live from *My Fair Lady* (1956, Broadway). Freddy Eynsford-Hill, a young man of no ambition in London's society who has accomplished nothing of his own, has fallen in love with Eliza Doolittle. Freddy is a dreamy guy who can think of nothing better to do than stand around in front of Eliza's house waiting for her to appear.

The Pirate King from *The Pirates of Penzance* (1879, New York). When Frederic, an indentured apprentice on a pirate ship, learns that he has served his full term, he wishes to return to civilization because he abhors the pirate lifestyle. He tries to convince the pirates to return with him, but the Pirate King refuses.

The Policeman's Song from *The Pirates of Penzance* (1879, New York). Mabel, Frederic's new love interest, informs the Sergeant of Police that the pirates are planning to take Frederic back into servitude. The Sergeant responds by singing a song about his lot in life.

Puttin' on the Ritz featured in *Blue Skies* (1946, film). This novelty song was written for a 1930 movie of the same title. The song is about regular folks pretending to be rich. A more famous performance on film was given by Clark Gable in the 1939 movie *Idiot's Delight* (excerpted in *That's Entertainment*).

River in the Rain from *Big River* (1985, film). Huckleberry Finn, on the run with Big Jim, sings this lonely ode to the Mississippi River.

Santa Fe from *Newsies* (1992, film). The movie is about newspaper boys in New York City around 1910. The seventeen year-old leader of the boys is an orphan. He has just visited a normal family's home for the first time in his life. He has heard beautiful things about Santa Fe which has become a mythical place in his mind.

Seize the Day from *Newsies* (1992, film). The newspaper boys in New York City in 1910 have been exploited. They have organized and are demanding fair treatment and worker's rights. This song is their anthem.

Sixteen Going on Seventeen from *The Sound of Music* (1959, Broadway). Rolf, the telegram delivery boy, sings this response to Liesl, a pretty girl on his route who has taken a liking to him.

Steppin' Out with My Baby from *Easter Parade* (1948, film). Most of the songs in this Irving Berlin score were anywhere from ten to twenty years old at the time the film was made. This snappy, big production number was a new song written for Fred Astaire.

The Surrey with the Fringe on Top from *Oklahoma!* (1943, Broadway). Curly is a cowhand in the turn of the century Oklahoma. In this song, he describes to his girlfriend, Laurey, what their date that evening will be like using imagery of the countryside. By all accounts, this was Oscar Hammerstein's favorite song in all his work.

Try to Remember from *The Fantasticks* (1960, Off-Broadway). The show is a timeless allegory. The narrator El Gallo starts the evening by addressing the audience in "Try to Remember."

Tschaikowsky from *Lady in the Dark* (1941, Broadway). All the numbers in this show are surreal, psychological dream sequences. In a circus scene, the ringmaster suddenly launches into a comic patter song about Russian composers.

Was I Wazir? from *Kismet* (1953, Broadway). In ancient Baghdad, the evil ruler is called the Wazir. In this song, we hear about his gruesome rule.

When I Was a Lad from *HMS Pinafore* (1878, London). On the ship, H.M.S. Pinafore, the captain has arranged for his daughter, Josephine, to be married to the First Lord of Admiralty, Sir Joseph Porter. She is not happy with the situation because she has fallen in love with a seaman on the ship. Sir Joseph Porter sings this short autobiographical sketch.

All I Need Is the Girl
from GYPSY

Words by STEPHEN SONDHEIM
Music by JULE STYNE

Copyright © 1959 by Norbeth Productions, Inc. and Stephen Sondheim
Copyright Renewed
All Rights Administered by Chappell & Co.
International Copyright Secured All Rights Reserved

7

Brush Up Your Shakespeare

from KISS ME, KATE

Words and Music by
COLE PORTER

The girls to-day in so-ci-e-ty Go for class-i-cal po-et-ry, So, to win their hearts, one must quote with ease Aes-chy-lus and Eu-ri-pi-

Copyright © 1949 by Cole Porter
Copyright Renewed, Assigned to John F. Wharton, Trustee of the Cole Porter Musical and Literary Property Trusts
Chappell & Co. owner of publication and allied rights throughout the world
International Copyright Secured   All Rights Reserved

pa - ter - er.
Cres - si - da,
on it.

And if still to be shocked she pre - tends, well,
If she says she won't buy it or tike* it,
When your ba - by is plead - ing for plea - sure

Just re - mind her that "All's Well That End's Well,"
Make her *tike it, what's more, As You Like It.
Let her sam - ple your "Mea - sure for Mea - sure."

Brush up your Shake - speare And they'll all kow -
Brush up your Shake - speare And they'll all kow -
Brush up your Shake - speare And they'll all kow -

tow! _____
tow! _____
tow! _____

* Cockney for take

Alone at the Drive-In Movie

from GREASE

Lyric and Music by WARREN CASEY
and JIM JACOBS

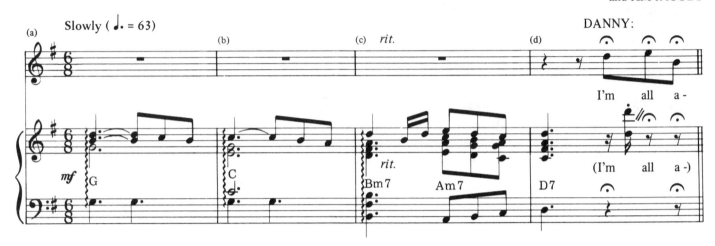

© 1971, 1972 WARREN CASEY and JIM JACOBS
All Rights Controlled by EDWIN H. MORRIS & COMPANY, A Division of MPL Communications, Inc.
All Rights Reserved

hold - ing the speak - er knobs, miss - ing you so._____ Can't be -

Cmaj7

Rhythm tacet

D7

lieve____ it,_____ un - steamed

G

C

win - dows__ I can see__ through,_____ might as

D7

G

C

The Bare Necessities
from Walt Disney's THE JUNGLE BOOK

Words and Music by
TERRY GILKYSON

Look for the bare ne - ces - si - ties, the

sim - ple bare ne - ces - si - ties; — for - get a - bout your

wor - ries and your strife.

I   mean   the
I   mean   the
I   mean   the

© 1964 Wonderland Music Company, Inc.
Copyright Renewed
International Copyright Secured   All Rights Reserved

Close Every Door

from JOSEPH AND THE AMAZING
TECHNICOLOR DREAMCOAT

Music by Andrew Lloyd Webber
Lyrics by Tim Rice

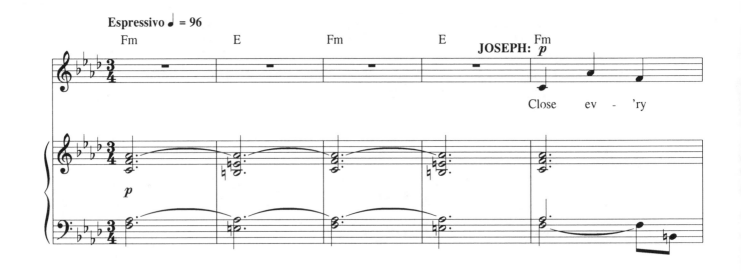

© Copyright 1969 The Really Useful Group Ltd.
All Rights for North America Controlled by Williamson Music Co.
International Copyright Secured   All Rights Reserved

The Farmer and the Cowman

from OKLAHOMA!

Lyrics by OSCAR HAMMERSTEIN II
Music by RICHARD RODGERS

Copyright © 1943 by WILLIAMSON MUSIC
Copyright Renewed
International Copyright Secured All Rights Reserved

Cow - boys dance with the farm - ers' daugh - ters, farm - ers dance with the

ran - chers' gals.

I'd like to say a word for the
I'd like to teach you all a lit - tle

farm - er: _____ He come out west and made a lot of
say - in', _____ and learn the words by heart the way you

Everybody Ought to Have a Maid

from A FUNNY THING HAPPENED ON THE WAY TO THE FORUM

Words and Music by
STEPHEN SONDHEIM

Copyright © 1962 by Stephen Sondheim
Copyright Renewed
Burthen Music Company, Inc., owner of publication and allied rights throughout the world
Chappell & Co., Sole Selling Agent
International Copyright Secured   All Rights Reserved

Friend Like Me

from Walt Disney's ALADDIN

Lyrics by HOWARD ASHMAN
Music by ALAN MENKEN

© 1992 Walt Disney Music Company and Wonderland Music Company, Inc.
International Copyright Secured   All Rights Reserved

Guys and Dolls
from GUYS AND DOLLS

Tune Uke
A D F♯ B

By FRANK LOESSER

Symbols for Guitar, Diagrams for Ukulele.

© 1950 (Renewed) FRANK MUSIC CORP.
All Rights Reserved

50

He Is an Englishman
from HMS PINAFORE

Words by WILLIAM S. GILBERT
Music by ARTHUR SULLIVAN

Copyright © 1997 by HAL LEONARD CORPORATION
International Copyright Secured   All Rights Reserved

52

Leaning on a Lamp-Post

from ME AND MY GIRL

Words and Music by
NOEL GAY

Copyright © 1937 (Renewed) Richard Armitage Ltd.
All Rights for the U.S. and Canada Controlled by Music Sales Corporation (ASCAP)
International Copyright Secured   All Rights Reserved
Reprinted by Permission

Les Poissons
from Walt Disney's THE LITTLE MERMAID

Lyrics by HOWARD ASHMAN
Music by ALAN MENKEN

© 1988 Walt Disney Music Company and Wonderland Music Company, Inc.
International Copyright Secured All Rights Reserved

Love, I Hear

from A FUNNY THING HAPPENED ON THE WAY TO THE FORUM

Words and Music by
STEPHEN SONDHEIM

Copyright © 1962 by Stephen Sondheim
Copyright Renewed
Burthen Music Company, Inc., owner of publication and allied rights throughout the world
Chappell & Co., Sole Selling Agent
International Copyright Secured   All Rights Reserved

Moderately - In 4

Love, I hear,_____ Makes you sigh a lot. Al - so,

love, I hear,_____ Leaves you weak._____

Love, I hear,_____ Makes you blush and turns you ash - en. You

try to speak with pas - sion and squeak, I hear.

know I am, I'm sure._ I mean, I hope I trust_ I pray_ I must_ Be

in! _____ For-

Tempo primo

give me if I shout._ For - give me if I crow._ I've

cn - ly just found out, And, well, I thought you ought to know. _

Luck Be a Lady
from GUYS AND DOLLS

Tune Uke
A D F♯ B

By FRANK LOESSER

Moderato

Piano

Voice

*G7+   C   G7+   C9

They call you Lad-y Luck but there is room for doubt At

F6 F♯dim C F9

times you have a ver-y un-lad-y-like way of run-ning out,— You're

G7+ C G7+ C9

on a date with me the pick-ings have been lush And

*Symbols for Guitar, Diagrams for Ukulele.

© 1950 (Renewed) FRANK MUSIC CORP.
All Rights Reserved

yet be-fore this eve-ning is ov-er you might give me the brush.__ You

might for-get your man-ners, you might re-fuse to stay, And so the best that I can do is

Brightly

pray.__

Chorus

Luck be a la-dy to-night _____

Nev - er get out of my sight_____

Stick with me ba - by I'm the fel - low you came in with,

Luck be a la - dy, luck be a la - dy, Luck be a la - dy to-night.

My Defenses Are Down

from the Stage Production ANNIE GET YOUR GUN

Words and Music by
IRVING BERLIN

© Copyright 1946 by Irving Berlin
Copyright Renewed
International Copyright Secured All Rights Reserved

On the Street Where You Live

from MY FAIR LADY

Words by ALAN JAY LERNER
Music by FREDERICK LOEWE

Copyright © 1956 by Alan Jay Lerner and Frederick Loewe
Copyright Renewed
Chappell & Co. owner of publication and allied rights throughout the world
International Copyright Secured   All Rights Reserved

The Pirate King

from THE PIRATES OF PENZANCE

Words by WILLIAM S. GILBERT
Music by ARTHUR SULLIVAN

1. Oh, better far to live and die Un-der the brave black flag I fly, Than play a sanc-ti-mo-nious part, With a pi-rate head and a pi-rate heart! A-

2. When I sal-ly forth to seek my prey, I help my-self in a roy-al way; I sink a few more ships it's true, Than a well-bred mon-arch ought to do! But

Copyright © 1997 by HAL LEONARD CORPORATION
International Copyright Secured   All Rights Reserved

85

86

Santa Fe

from Walt Disney's NEWSIES

Lyrics by JACK FELDMAN
Music by ALAN MENKEN

Freely

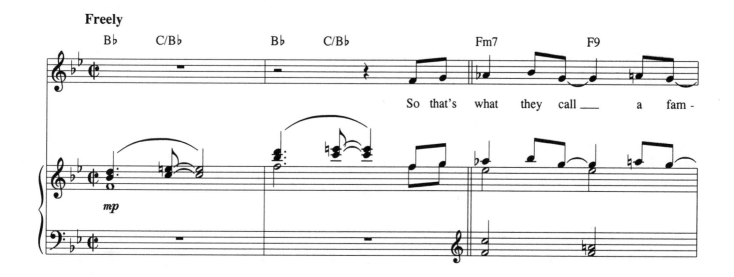

So that's what they call __ a fam -

- 'ly __ moth - er, daugh - ter, __ fa - ther, son. __ Guess that

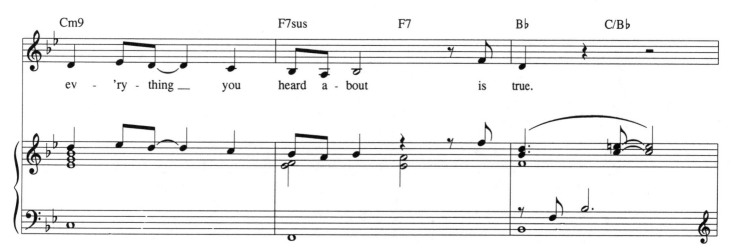

ev - 'ry - thing __ you heard a - bout is true.

© 1992 Wonderland Music Company, Inc.
International Copyright Secured   All Rights Reserved

94

The Policeman's Song
from THE PIRATES OF PENZANCE

Words by WILLIAM S. GILBERT
Music by ARTHUR SULLIVAN

Copyright © 1997 by HAL LEONARD CORPORATION
International Copyright Secured   All Rights Reserved

Puttin' on the Ritz
featured in the Motion Picture BLUE SKIES

Words and Music by
IRVING BERLIN

© Copyright 1928, 1929 by Irving Berlin
© Arrangement Copyright 1946 by Irving Berlin
Copyright Renewed
International Copyright Secured   All Rights Reserved

River in the Rain
from BIG RIVER

Music and Lyrics by
ROGER MILLER

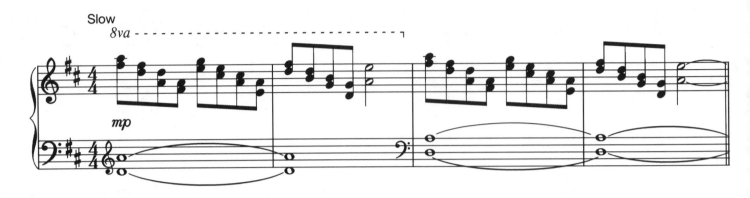

Copyright © 1985 Sony/ATV Songs LLC and Roger Miller Music
All Rights Administered by Sony/ATV Music Publishing, 8 Music Square West, Nashville, TN 37203
International Copyright Secured   All Rights Reserved

107

Seize the Day
from Walt Disney's NEWSIES

Lyrics by JACK FELDMAN
Music by ALAN MENKEN

© 1992 Wonderland Music Company, Inc.
International Copyright Secured All Rights Reserved

112

C Dm/C C Am G F
(Don't be a-fraid and don't de-lay.) Noth - ing can break us. No one can make us
G7 C Am C7/G
give our rights a - way. Neigh-bor to
F G Asus
neigh - bor, fa - ther to son
A/C♯ Dm C/E F G C
one for all and all for one.

Sixteen Going on Seventeen

from THE SOUND OF MUSIC

Lyrics by OSCAR HAMMERSTEIN II
Music by RICHARD RODGERS

Copyright © 1959 by Richard Rodgers and Oscar Hammerstein II
Copyright Renewed
WILLIAMSON MUSIC owner of publication and allied rights throughout the world
International Copyright Secured   All Rights Reserved

Steppin' Out with My Baby

from the Motion Picture Irving Berlin's EASTER PARADE

Words and Music by
IRVING BERLIN

© Copyright 1947 by Irving Berlin
Copyright Renewed
International Copyright Secured All Rights Reserved

The Surrey with the Fringe on Top

from OKLAHOMA!

Lyrics by OSCAR HAMMERSTEIN II
Music by RICHARD RODGERS

Brightly

When I take you out, to-night, with me,

Hon - ey, here's the way it's goin' to be:

You will set be - hind a team of snow - white hors - es,

Copyright © 1943 by WILLIAMSON MUSIC
Copyright Renewed
International Copyright Secured   All Rights Reserved

Try to Remember
from THE FANTASTICKS

Words by TOM JONES
Music by HARVEY SCHMIDT

Moderato

Piano

Refrain *(Slowly, with tenderness)*

1. Try to re-mem-ber the kind of Sep-tem-ber when
2. Try to re-mem-ber when life was so ten-der that
3. Deep in De-cem-ber it's nice to re-mem-ber al-

life was slow and oh, so mel-low.
no one wept ex-cept the wil-low.
tho' you know the snow will fol-low.

Copyright © 1960 by Tom Jones and Harvey Schmidt
Copyright Renewed
Chappell & Co. owner of publication and allied rights throughout the world
International Copyright Secured   All Rights Reserved

Tschaikowsky
(And Other Russians)
from the Musical Production LADY IN THE DARK

Words by IRA GERSHWIN
Music by KURT WEILL

There's Ma - li - chev - sky, Ru - ben - stein, A -
ren - sky and Tschai - kow - sky, Sa - pel - ni - koff, Di - mit - ri - eff, Tsche -

TRO - © Copyright 1941 (Renewed) Hampshire House Publishing Corp., New York and Chappell & Co.
International Copyright Secured
All Rights Reserved Including Public Performance For Profit
Used by Permission

rep - nin, Kry - ja - now - sky, Go - dow - sky, Ar - tei - bou - cheff, Mo - ni -

usz - ko, A - ki - men - ko, So - lo - vi - eff, Pro - ko - fi - eff, Ti -

om - kin, Ko - rest - chen - ko. There's Glin - ka, Wink - ler, Bort - ni - an - sky,

Re - bi - koff, Il - yin - sky, There's Medt - ner, Ba - la - kir - eff, Zo - lo -

132

Was I Wazir?

from KISMET

Words and Music by ROBERT WRIGHT
and GEORGE FORREST
(Music Based on Themes of A. BORODIN)

"Wazir" is the wicked ruler of an Arab nation.

Copyright © 1953 Frank Music Corp.
Copyright Renewed and Assigned to Scheffel Music Corp., New York, NY
All Rights Controlled by Scheffel Music Corp.
All Rights Reserved   International Copyright Secured

138

When I Was a Lad

from HMS PINAFORE

Words by William S. Gilbert
Music by Arthur Sullivan

Allegro non troppo

SIR J. PORTER:

1. When I was a lad I served a term As of-fice boy to an At-tor-ney's firm, I cleaned the win-dows and I swept the floor, And I
2. As of-fice boy I made such a mark That they gave me the post of a ju-nior clerk. I served the writs with a smile so bland, And I

Copyright © 1996 by HAL LEONARD CORPORATION
International Copyright Secured   All Rights Reserved

polished up the han - dle of the big front door.
copied all the let - ters in a big round hand.

I po - lished up that han - dle so care - ful - lee, That
I co - pied all the let - ters in a hand so free, That

now I am the ru - ler of the Queen's Na - vee!
now I am the ru - ler of the Queen's Na - vee!

3. In ser - ving writs I made such a name That an
4. Of le - gal know-ledge I ac - quired such a grip That they

ar - ti - cled clerk I___ soon be - came; I wore clean col - lars and a bran' new suit For the
took me in - to the part - ner - ship, And that jun - ior part - ner - ship I ween Was the

pass ex - am - in - a - tion at the In - sti - tute. That
on - ly ship___ that I ev - er had seen. But

pass ex - am - in - a - tion did so well for me } That now I am the ru - ler of the Queen's Na - vee.
that kind of ship so suit - ed me }

5. I grew so rich that I was sent By a
6. Now lands-men all, who - ev - er you may be, If you

pock - et bor - ough in - to Par - lia - ment. I al - ways vo - ted at my
want to rise ___ to the top of the tree, If your soul is - n't fet - tered to an

par - ty's call, And I nev - er thought of think-ing for my - self at all.
of - fice stool, Be care-ful to be guid-ed by this gold - en rule,

I thought so lit-tle, they re-ward-ed me, By
Stick close to your desks and nev-er go to sea, And you

mak-ing me the ru-ler of the Queen's Na - vee.
all may be ru-lers of the Queen's Na - vee.